PAST & PRESENT

WALLA WALLA

OPPOSITE: This photograph from 1918 looks east toward the busy intersection of Main Street and First Avenue. The local *Up to the Times* magazine stated in 1909 that there were 60 automobiles in Walla Walla. Obviously, ownership increased significantly in the nine years following. There are no streetcars vying with automobiles for the right-of-way today, but Main Street is still lively. (Whitman College Archives.)

WALLA WALLA

Susan Monahan

I dedicate this book to my mother, Doris Monahan—a historian and author herself—who instilled a love of history in me and would have been so pleased about my writing this book.

Copyright © 2022 by Susan Monahan
ISBN 978-1-4671-0810-2

Library of Congress Control Number: 2021952354

Published by Arcadia Publishing
Charleston, South Carolina

Printed in the United States of America

For all general information, please contact Arcadia Publishing:
Telephone 843-853-2070
Fax 843-853-0044
E-mail sales@arcadiapublishing.com
For customer service and orders:
Toll-Free 1-888-313-2665

Visit us on the Internet at www.arcadiapublishing.com

ON THE FRONT COVER: One of Walla Walla's most photographed buildings, the Liberty Theater was designed by Henry Osterman and constructed in 1917. The front's gleaming white surface is faced with glazed terra-cotta tile and adorned with eagles. Originally named the American, the theater was equipped with an organ, which accompanied silent films. Later, the theater offered "talkies." The last film to be shown at the Liberty Theater was in the 1980s. It is retail space today. (Past image, Whitman College Archives; present image, Steve Wilen.

ON THE BACK COVER: Built in 1905 at Fourth Avenue and Poplar Street by Mordo McDonald, this imposing brick livery stable housed 75 horses on three floors. McDonald was a well-known horse dealer and breeder in Walla Walla and provided horses to the government for service in the Philippines. Yellow paint was removed, the grand building lovingly restored, and its signs refreshed in 2013. A salon and tasting room occupy the building today. (Fort Walla Walla Museum.)

CONTENTS

Acknowledgments

While writing this book, I have had the help and support of several people who are also passionate about the history of the fascinating town of Walla Walla. My good friend and fellow history enthusiast and author Steve Wilen was responsible for all the "present" photographs, which meant standing in the middle of potentially busy intersections, climbing ladders to get an accurate viewpoint, and waiting patiently for just the right light. He contributed ideas regarding architectural details and was also generous with his extensive postcard collection. Jeanne McMenemy cheerfully and skillfully scanned all those postcards and other photographs. Whitman College Archives bent over backwards to provide me with historic photographs; Dana Bronson, the archivist there, was especially helpful. Fort Walla Walla Museum was another source for photographs, and Blake Cheneweth was always willing to locate and scan images. When I needed more information about a building or to look at different views and perspectives, I went to Joe Drazan's website where thousands of historic photographs of structures and artifacts of Walla Walla are made available to everyone. My husband, Mark Brucks, has read every word I have ever written. He catches typos, makes suggestions for clarification and syntax, and is consistently encouraging and supportive of my writing efforts.

Arcadia Publishing was patient and helpful during the long process from start to finish.

All present photographs in this book were taken by Steve Wilen.

INTRODUCTION

The goal of this book is to offer the reader a sample of historic and current images that tell some of the story of the rich history of Walla Walla, a small but significant town tucked in the southeastern corner of Washington. The time elapsed between a past and a present image of a building or street scene is in some cases as much as 154 years. Some past images are vintage photographs or engravings, and some are historic postcards.

Walla Walla's name is said to mean "Land of Many Waters," but it would be even more appropriate to call it the land of many cultures and many stories. The native tribes of Cayuse, Walla Walla, Umatilla, Palouse, and Nez Perce were here long before settlers of European origin. Lewis and Clark came through the Walla Walla Valley on their expedition and provided early records of the people and wildlife of the area. They relied on Indian trails to find their way out of the valley.

Some assume that the missionaries Narcissa and Marcus Whitman, who arrived in 1836, were the first settlers in the area, but French trappers and explorers, whose wives were often Native American women, had established the Frenchtown community with their families as early as 1823. Locals and visitors have numerous opportunities to learn about Walla Walla's earliest history. Whitman Mission is a national historic site where one can see the outline of original buildings and learn about mission and native life from displays in the museum. Featured at the Frenchtown historic site are interpretive signs, a cemetery, and what is believed to be the oldest example of French-Canadian construction in Washington state, the recently restored Prince's Cabin.

As a result of a gold rush in Idaho in the 1860s, Walla Walla was for a while the largest community in the Territory of Washington. Early prosperity was achieved by merchants who supplied prospectors headed for the Idaho gold mines. At one point, Walla Walla was slated to be the new state's capital. Another important cultural layer was added when Chinese people came to the valley. At first, they headed toward the Idaho mines but later returned to Walla Walla to work on railroads and finally settled in town and became merchants, laundrymen, and domestics. The Chinese were also productive truck gardeners, as were the Italians who settled here in the late 1880s. A stroll through Fort Walla Walla Museum's Pioneer Village offers a taste of life in and around Walla Walla in the late 1800s and early 1900s. Encircling a common area, 17 structures ranging from cabins and a school to a blacksmith shop and shaving parlor have been moved to the site and are filled with authentic furnishings and artifacts.

The community's agricultural heritage is as rich as the soil. Walla Walla eventually became the center of extensive wheat and vegetable farming and developed food-processing and lumber industries. The spring and summer fields of the valley are resplendent with wheat, and the local farmers market offers the sweet onions for which Walla Walla is famous.

Agriculture, mercantile, and railroads created fortunes, and wealthy folks constructed grand houses and public buildings. This book presents examples of the elegant homes and buildings that have been preserved, but one must always keep in mind that historic places were not always venerated just because of their age. The current present photographs paired with the past images do not represent that time in between when buildings were "modernized" before being renovated, restored, and repurposed. One does not see the awkward age of the 1960s, 1970s, and 1980s, when facades covered elegant Victorian Italianate arched windows or mansions were carved up into apartment buildings. The reality is that some of the most elegant buildings downtown and grand homes in neighborhoods have been razed. Three casualties of "progress" versus preservation: the Blalock-Dooley Mansion, the White Temple Baptist Church, and the Stencel Building. The three are featured as chapter heading photographs to remind us of the beauty of these bygone structures.

Walla Wallans rediscovered their architectural treasures in the 1990s, and the past three decades have seen energetic efforts to restore and preserve. During the downtown revitalization of the 1990s, businesses that had left the city returned to restored retail spaces, and new enterprises started. In 2001, Walla Walla was a Great American Main Street Award winner due to the transformation and preservation of its once deteriorated and deserted Main Street.

The community prides itself that of the 33 Walla Walla County properties listed in the National Register of Historic Places, 24 are within the city limits. The Walla Walla 2020 Historic Sites & Markers Project honors previously unrecognized Walla Walla area historic sites, many of which may have been unknown to the general public, by erecting interpretive signage and providing additional details about their significance. The locations of long gone but historically important structures such as the Chinese Building and Baker School have been marked by Walla Walla 2020 with interpretive signs.

Walla Walla's wine industry receives national attention. Wineries and tasting facilities—there are over 120 in the area—bring tourists, especially from Seattle and Portland. Several repurposed historic buildings such as the former McDonald's Livery Stable and Whitehouse Crawford Planing Mill now house winery tasting rooms. The now inactive World War II air base features winery tasting rooms among former military barracks and communal buildings.

Visitors who come to Walla Walla to taste and purchase wine are charmed by historic Main Street and the nearby neighborhoods whose streets are lined with lovely homes. Walking tour brochures created by the Walla Walla Downtown Foundation allow for leisurely and informative self-guided tours through downtown, historic neighborhoods, Pioneer Park, and Fort Walla Walla.

I am proud to live in a place where our rich history is valued and the buildings that reflect that history are honored. What a privilege it is to have the opportunity to share some of my favorite historic buildings with others through this book.

BUSINESS

The narrow and ornate Stencel Building was designed by George Babcock and stood on the southeast corner of Main Street and Third Avenue. Built in 1890, it housed a variety of businesses. Unfortunately, not all old buildings are preserved; the Stencel Building was razed in the 1960s and a small, paved park now occupies the space. (Past image, Whitman College Archives.)

One of Walla Walla's most photographed buildings, the Liberty Theater on Main Street was designed by Henry Osterman and built in 1917. The front's gleaming white surface is faced with glazed terra-cotta tile and adorned with eagles. Originally named the American, the theater was equipped with an organ, which accompanied silent films. Later, the theater offered "talkies." The last film to be shown at the Liberty Theater was in the 1980s. It is retail space today. (Past image, Whitman College Archives.)

The Paine Building at the corner of Second Avenue and Main Street was constructed in 1879 by brothers Frank and John Paine, farm implements dealers. The building housed the First National Bank and a variety of businesses, including the barbershop of Jamaican-born Richard Bogle.

John Paine resided in a third-floor suite. On the top floor, the US Weather Service set up Walla Walla's first weather station in 1885. The exterior of the building has recently been restored. (Past image, Whitman College Archives.)

Pacific Telephone and Telegraph Co. Bldg.   Walla Walla   Was

In a town of redbrick Italianate-style architecture, the gold brick Art Deco building at First Avenue and Alder Street stands out. It was constructed in 1935 by the Pacific Telephone and Telegraph Company, which was located in a smaller building nearby and had an immediate need for more room for its equipment. Building began in August and was completed by December. Today, it houses a cell phone company. (Past image, Whitman College Archives.)

This 1906 building on the corner of Colville and Alder Streets was originally one story; the second story and mission-style roofline were added in 1913. Built by funeral directors McMartin and Hill, it contained a chapel with an organ and a casket showroom. Today housing a florist, the building has been used as a thrift store and a beauty school, but as a reminder of its past, an engraving on the sidewalk marks the chapel entrance. (Past image, Whitman College Archives.)

The First National Bank was established in Walla Walla by Levi Ankeny in 1878. Ankeny beat Dorsey Baker and John Boyer by just a few days in registering First National Bank in Washington, DC, making it the first federally registered bank in Walla Walla. In 1920, First National Bank moved to this impressive new building on Alder Street, designed in the Classical Revival style by the twin Beezer brothers, Louis and Michael. It houses a bank today. (Past image, Steve Wilen.)

1590. First National Bank, Walla Walla, Wash.

Built in 1905 at Fourth Avenue and Poplar Street by Mordo McDonald, this imposing brick livery stable housed 75 horses on three floors. McDonald was a well-known horse dealer and breeder in Walla Walla and provided horses to the government for service in the Philippines. In 2013, the yellow paint was removed, the grand building lovingly restored, and its signs refreshed. A salon and tasting room occupy the building today. (Past image, Fort Walla Walla Museum.)

This building on Main Street and Fourth Avenue was originally the Stine Hotel but suffered a disastrous fire in 1889. In 1910, a total of $25,000 was spent on its restoration, and it reopened as the Dacres Hotel. Offering a tailor shop, a barbershop, and Turkish baths, the building also had a ladies' grill, a men's grill, and a café. Featuring plush carpets and potted palms, the Dacres provided truly luxurious lodging. Today, the Dacres hosts music events. (Past image, Steve Wilen.)

Founded in 1880 by J.M. Crawford, Whitehouse-Crawford Planing Mill created milled lumber for canneries, churches, and Whitman College buildings. It also manufactured showcases, storefronts, and fixtures for downtown businesses. The display cases still used by Tallman's Pharmacy were made by Whitehouse-Crawford. The 1904 building that still stands on Third Avenue was sold to the City of Walla Walla in 1988. It is listed in the National Register of Historic Places and has been converted to restaurant space. (Past image, Whitman College Archives.)

What is called the Jones Building today was known as the Rees Winans Building when it was designed by George Babcock in 1890. The original grand towered building housed a bank and offices, but upstairs was also the home of the Walla Walla Club, which provided a place for men to read newspapers, discuss current events, and smoke cigars. The ornate and elaborate Rees Winans Building underwent a severe modernization in 1951. (Past image, Whitman College Archives.)

General Hospital, Walla-Walla, Wash.

In 1925, a group of local doctors built Walla Walla General Hospital on Bonsella Street. The hospital fell on hard times financially, and in 1931, it was bought by the Upper Columbia Conference of Seventh-day Adventists, who operated it until they moved to a new facility on Second Avenue in 1977. Changes were made when Whitman College remodeled the hospital to create the North Hall dormitory, but the college preserved the wide halls, large rooms, parklike grounds, and pond. (Past image, Steve Wilen.)

The 1880 photograph shows the Reynolds-Day Building at Main Street and Second Avenue. The left side of the first floor was the former location of A.H. Reynolds's bank, and the right side had originally been the pharmacy of J.H. Day. Upstairs were professional offices and the site of the Washington Constitutional Convention of 1878. The building was painstakingly restored in the 1990s, and today, a jeweler and a restaurant occupy the first-floor spaces. (Past image, Whitman College Archives.)

Marcy's was opened as a Union 76 station in 1935 and was situated near Walla Walla's "Auto Row" on Alder Street. The station was advertised by owner Milo Marcy as offering complete automotive servicing to the numerous nearby dealerships. The gas pumps were removed some time ago, and the Art Deco–style building has been home to numerous businesses. It is still called Marcy's today but serves food and drinks instead of repairing automobiles. (Past image, Whitman College Archives.)

Behind the glazed white tiles of the building at the northwest corner of Main Street and Second Avenue is a brick structure dating from 1878. Originally it housed a mercantile, then a pharmacy, and then the Third National Bank. It was the bank that enhanced the building with its new facade in 1920. An office building today, it has been the site of several cafés, including the Corner Café, which closed in 1974. (Past image, Whitman College Archives.)

Third National Bank Walla Walla, Wash.

BUSINESS

When Logan Chevrolet was first constructed in 1930 on the corner of Poplar Street and Second Avenue, the dealership was an unpainted brick building. Carl and Jack Logan sold Chevrolets and Cadillacs, and a fixture at their store was Bob "the Chevrolet Dog." During the 1931 Mill Creek flood, Logan Chevrolet was inundated. Inland Printing later occupied the building, and since that company left, it has been used as an art gallery. (Past image, Whitman College Archives.)

Because it was the first concrete structure in town, the Roberts Monument Company on Main Street was both unique and controversial. It was designed by Lee W. Roberts, a member of a family who had been in the stone monument business since 1872. The firm was responsible for memorials in Mountain View Cemetery and around town, including the Spanish-American soldier statue in Volunteer Park. Housing offices today, the building retains the arches from its past. (Past image, Whitman College Archives.)

Max Baumeister erected this building in 1889. One of a few metal-fronted buildings in downtown Walla Walla, its facade was ordered from the catalog of Mesker Brothers Ironworks of St. Louis. Originally shops below and offices and furnished rooms on the second floor, the building housed a variety of businesses over the years. Restored in 1998, the Baumeister Building is listed in the National Register of Historic Places. It is office and retail space today. (Past image, Whitman College Archives.)

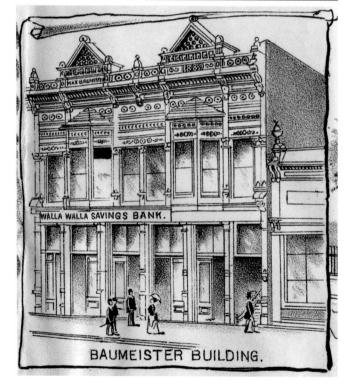

This building on West Alder Street was the Ennis family residence in 1889, but by 1910, E.S. Hennessey had moved his funeral home here. Other partners over the years included Lewis Calloway and Dock Marshall. During World War II, the funeral home had the casualty contract with Walla Walla's Army air base where training sometimes resulted in crashes. Norman Herring assumed ownership in 1950. The Herring Funeral Home is now in its third generation of family ownership. (Past image, Whitman College Archives.)

LOWAY-HENNESSEY FUNERAL HOME, WALLA WALLA, WASH.

Eugene Tausick, the owner of Walla Walla Steam Laundry, was a household name in early Walla Walla. He was mayor and owned a lumberyard, an ice company, and two elegant hotels. In his spare time, he directed the county fair. The brick laundry he erected on Fourth Avenue and Rose Street replaced a frame structure. By 1907, Tausick employed 60 men and women as ironers, starchers, folders, and manglers. (Past image, Whitman College Archives.)

WALLA WALLA'S LARGEST DEPARTMENT STORE.

The 1906 Denny Building on Alder Street and Second Avenue was designed by Henry Osterman for Arthur Denny, a Seattle capitalist. Originally, it housed the Hanger and Thompson Department Store, which prided itself on its quality merchandise, ladies' lounge, and brass Lamson cash carrier that transported money and receipts between floors. Downstairs at the Denny was so spacious that it hosted auto shows and other exhibits. Today, the restored Denny Building houses offices. (Past image, Steve Wilen.)

John Stoller and Robert Wentsch constructed this building in 1919 for their Pantorium Cleaners, which had been located across the street. They shared their space with numerous other businesses over the years, including a café, a shoeshine stand, a photography studio, and a barbershop. One could still take dry cleaning to Pantorium until 1988. A 2005 restoration revealed the charm of the original building. Today, it houses the tasting room for a local winery. (Past image, Whitman College Archives.)

The Drumheller family settled in Walla Walla in 1859 and sons Oscar and Tom began the Drumheller Company in 1904 on Second Avenue and Alder Street. An elevator with an attendant took customers and clients to the upper floors where doctors, lawyers, and architects had their offices. Drumheller's is remembered fondly as a department store where one could buy hardware, sports equipment, furniture, and even Oriental rugs. The store closed in 1984 and is office space today. (Past image, Whitman College Archives.)

CHAPTER 2

CHURCHES
AND SCHOOLS

401. White Temple, First Baptist Church
Walla Walla, Wash.

The Classic Revival–style White Baptist Temple Church was built in 1912 on the southwest corner of Boyer Avenue and Park Street. As part of his 1913 fundraising tour for the Tuskegee Institute, Booker T. Washington addressed an audience of 1,300 in the sanctuary. Razed in 1986, the church was replaced by the Reid Campus Center at Whitman College. (Steve Wilen.)

The imposing Central Christian Church on Palouse and Alder Streets was dedicated in 1892 with much fanfare. The railroad transported attendees from the nearby towns of Dayton, Waitsburg, and Dixie for the event. The church's stained-glass windows were designed by the Povey Brothers, who produced distinctive windows for many churches in the Northwest. In a pocket-sized city park adjoining the church is a statue dedicated to the veterans of the Spanish-American War. (Past image, Whitman College Archives.)

CHURCHES AND SCHOOLS

The First Congregational Church that stood previously on this site on Palouse and Alder Streets burned to the ground. The current church, dedicated in 1931, was designed by Arnott Woodroofe. Its spire is clad with copper and is visible all over town. The location of the church and its parish hall provides for an unobstructed view looking east on Alder Street, making the buildings two of Walla Walla's most photographed structures. (Past image, Steve Wilen.)

First Congregational Church

Photo: Lynn Callen

Its design inspired by a church in Bavaria, St. Paul's Episcopal Church was created by Spokane architect Kirtland Cutter and consecrated in 1906. The Catherine Street church has had its share of disasters. In 1907, the east end of the church was destroyed by fire. The destructive flood of 1931 deposited a thick layer of mud and debris throughout the building, but church members raised money for repairs. The parish hall was added in 1955. (Past image, Steve Wilen.)

509 – ST. PAUL'S EPISCOPAL CHURCH, WALLA WALLA, WASHINGTON.

CHURCHES AND SCHOOLS

Roman Catholic Church, Walla Walla, Wash.

The first Catholic church in Walla Walla was built in 1859, and a second one was constructed in the 1860s. This past image shows the third church, St. Patrick's, as it appeared when dedicated on Christmas Day 1881. The Gothic-style brick church at Seventh Avenue and Alder Street is part of a complex of church buildings that occupy an entire city block. St. Patrick's was listed in the National Register of Historic Places in 1995. (Past image, Steve Wilen.)

Built in 1912, the First Presbyterian Church on the corner of First Avenue and Birch Street is one of Walla Walla's stately stone churches. This church replaced a frame structure just across the street and incorporated the Cumberland Presbyterian Church congregation. The builders were architect Charles Lambert, a Swede, and contractor Charles Bailey, a Canadian, who were responsible for several of Walla Walla's public structures and many homes. (Past image, Steve Wilen.)

CHURCHES AND SCHOOLS

"Thoroughly modern in every respect" was how the *Evening Statesman* described Washington School when it was built on Cayuse Street in 1901. There was a class for each grade from first to sixth. A barn on the property housed the principal's horse and buggy. The last school bell rang in 1982, but the building was remodeled by the Walla Walla Housing Authority and offers 24 one-bedroom apartments. The building is listed in the National Register of Historic Places. (Past image, Whitman College Archives.)

WASHINGTON PUBLIC SCHOOL WALLA WALLA, WASH. USA

CHURCHES AND SCHOOLS

Whitman College's Hunter Conservatory on Boyer Avenue and Park Street was originally called MacDowell Hall and was dedicated in 1910. The building was designed to house the Whitman Conservatory of Music. It provided classroom space, office space, practice rooms, and an Otis elevator that could carry pianos to each floor from the tuning room in the basement. The auditorium is in use today as an intimate space for concerts. (Past image, Whitman College Archives.)

Built in 1898 and named after Benjamin Sharpstein, a local judge, Sharpstein School on Whitman and Park Streets has educated students for over a century. Its architect, Henry Osterman, juxtaposed squared blocks of stone with smooth surfaces on the building's exterior, an architectural design trend labeled "rustication." A compatible new addition and interior renovation in the early 2000s allowed the school to be preserved. (Past image, Whitman College Archives.)

Named for a donor to Whitman College, Billings Hall was originally built in 1899 to be a men's dormitory, but was converted to the Science Hall in 1914. The bridge seen in both the past and present photographs was a gift of alumni and was built to provide a shortcut over College Creek in 1918. Billings Hall was razed in 1972 and the footbridge now leads to Maxey Hall. (Past image, Whitman College Archives.)

CHURCHES AND SCHOOLS

The 1905 Green Park School on East Isaacs Avenue was built as part of Green's Park Addition, a development constructed on ground that had for 40 years been farmed by Chinese gardeners. According to the *Evening Statesman*, Henry Osterman, the architect, was "compelled to work almost day and night" on the plans for the Dutch Colonial building, which was constructed of brick from Weston, Oregon, and stone from the Tenino quarries near Olympia. It still serves as an elementary school. (Past image, Steve Wilen.)

Built in 1899 and designed by George Babcock, Memorial Hall on Boyer Avenue is the tallest structure on the Whitman College campus. In 1903, Pres. Theodore Roosevelt spoke to a large crowd from its porch. In the past, "Mem" housed the library, science labs, and the college chapel. Today, it is administrative offices. The Memorial Hall clock tower chimes 180 times a day. Memorial Hall was listed in the National Register of Historic Places in 1974. (Past image, Steve Wilen.)

Whitman Memorial Building, Walla Walla, Wash.

CHURCHES AND SCHOOLS

ORGANIZATIONS AND PUBLIC PLACES

2247   Elks Temple, Walla Walla, Wash.

The Beaux-Arts Elks Lodge stood at Fourth Avenue and Alder Street for 60 years but was razed in 1973 after a disastrous fire. The Elks offered club rooms and rooms for banquets, billiards, and reading. The huge bronze elk that stood on the roof was salvaged and found a new home at the new Elks Lodge. (Steve Wilen.)

Facing Fifth Street, the fireproof Hall of Records storage facility, which is still in use, was constructed in 1891 by builder Norman Francis Butler. Its smooth surface was achieved by covering pressed bricks with plaster. The concrete surrounds of the entrance and dramatic hooded windows are formed to give the appearance of stone blocks. In the past photograph there is an older courthouse in the background; that building was replaced by a grand new courthouse in 1917. (Past image, Whitman College Archives.)

ORGANIZATIONS AND PUBLIC PLACES

On the corner of Alder and Colville Streets, this elegant 1905 brick Masonic Temple in the Beaux-Arts style was designed by Henry Osterman. The building had designated meeting space on the upper floors while businesses operated at ground level. The Masons moved to a new home in 1952. Today, the upper story is home to a dance studio and bookstore; downstairs is a popular bakery. (Past image, Steve Wilen.)

Since it was built in 1919, the armory on the corner of Colville and Poplar Streets has housed the National Guard. Henry Osterman and Victor Siebert were the architects. The armory was an especially lively place during World War II when it hosted films and dances. The bus stop for the air base was just outside. Bored servicemen sometimes scratched graffiti into the red bricks, which can still be seen today. (Past image, Whitman College Archives.)

ORGANIZATIONS AND PUBLIC PLACES

The City Cemetery opened in 1853. It was divided into three separate areas owned by the Masonic Lodge, Independent Order of Odd Fellows, and the Catholic Church. Those sections have now been unified and the name changed to Mountain View Cemetery. A tobacco can time capsule was discovered during repairs of a pillar at the main gate containing a newspaper from 1930, which confirms the year the pillars and wrought iron gate were built. (Past image, Whitman College Archives.)

Walla Walla's 1905 former library on Palouse and Alder Streets is one of the 1,700 Carnegie libraries nationwide. Some were ornate, but most in small towns were fairly simple in design. Local architect Henry Osterman patterned Walla Walla's library after a similar one in Wellington, Ohio. After it outgrew its space, the library moved into a new building in 1970 and the Carnegie building became an art center. (Past image, Fort Walla Walla Museum.)

ORGANIZATIONS AND PUBLIC PLACES

Repurposing the 1902 Odd Fellows building is an inspiring example of saving a building headed for demolition. In 1993, the organization ArtWalla took on the project of dismantling, moving, and reconstructing the top stories of the facade of the former Alder Street Odd Fellows lodge. Now installed in Heritage Park on Main Street, it has been transformed into a mural called *Windows on the Past*. Each window contains an enameled panel representing one of the myriad cultures of Walla Walla. (Past image, Jeanne McMenemy.)

Ransom Clark built this cabin on his homestead in 1858 but died before he was able to live there. His plucky widow, Lettice, journeyed up the Columbia River with their children to "prove up" the claim and finish the cabin. Lettice moved into a frame house after her second marriage to mill-owner A.H. Reynolds. The spacious cabin—with two living areas separated by a breezeway—was moved to Fort Walla Walla Museum in 1969. (Past image, Library of Congress.)

ORGANIZATIONS AND PUBLIC PLACES

Walla Walla's post office, now at Second Avenue and Sumach Street, had several locations over the years. The 1914 brick Federal Building originally housed the post office on the first floor and a courthouse (now office space) on the second. For many years there was a Lions Club–sponsored concession in the lobby run by a visually impaired person aided by a guide dog. The building was listed in the National Register of Historic Places in 1991. (Past image, Whitman College Archives.)

The vacant storefront on West Main Street is quiet today, but during World War II it was the United Service Organization's club for African American servicemen and Women's Army Corps (WACs) stationed at Walla Walla's air base. Blacks were segregated at the air base and local businesses did not always welcome them, so the so-called "separate but equal" USO was an especially important gathering place. There was a USO for white servicemen a few blocks away on Alder Street. (Past image, Fort Walla Walla Museum.)

ORGANIZATIONS AND PUBLIC PLACES

Built in 1916, the courthouse shown in the past image replaced one that occupied the same spot on the square on Main Street but was deemed unsafe. Henry Osterman traveled around the Northwest to look at other courthouses and claimed the new one he designed with partner Victor Siebert included all the best elements of those he visited. Still in use today, the Classical Revival–style courthouse is constructed of steel and concrete faced with limestone. (Past image, Steve Wilen.)

1602. Court House, Walla Wal'a, Wash.

Walla Walla's main park was designed by John Langdon, a local businessman, and was financed by the tireless efforts of the Women's Park Club, headed by Grace Isaacs. The club held numerous balls, card parties, and performances, and sold "For A City Park" lapel buttons for $1 to fund the park. In 1908, the park had its formal opening; its bandstand was built in 1909. In 1931, City Park became Pioneer Park. (Past image, Steve Wilen.)

1613. City Park, Walla Walla, Wash.

ORGANIZATIONS AND PUBLIC PLACES

CHAPTER 4

STREET SCENES

The homes seen in this photograph were the first to be built on Alvarado Terrace during the development of Green's Park Addition, which began in 1904. The neighborhood was created on ground that had formerly been farmed by Chinese truck gardeners, who lost their leases and had to seek plots in other parts of town. (Whitman College Archives.)

Looking east toward the intersection of Sixth Avenue and Main Street, the past image shows streetcars that were part of an interurban electric railway that began in 1906. Twelve miles of tracks formed a loop in the central portion of the city. The old courthouse is seen on the right; on the northeast corner was a streetcar depot featuring a comfortable waiting room. Streetcars stopped running in 1931, and the former depot is now a restaurant. (Past image, Fort Walla Walla Museum.)

STREET SCENES

The postcard creator was not able to spell "Valencia" correctly, but did capture a charming street scene on a winter morning. Valencia is a street in the Green's Park Addition, which was platted by Mary Green in 1903. In order to avoid speculative building, the Green family stipulated that houses built in the addition must cost at least $2,000, which resulted in the stately stretch of homes seen here. (Past image, Steve Wilen.)

A Frosty Morning on Valancia Street, Walla Walla, Wash.

Second Avenue and Main Street is Walla Walla's busiest downtown intersection. The white building on the corner in the past image was a restaurant at the time, but today it is office space. Walla Walla's skyscraper, the Marcus Whitman Hotel, towers as it has since 1928. When the hotel was constructed, a city ordinance was passed stating that no other structure could be built taller than the Marcus Whitman Hotel. (Past image, Steve Wilen.

Lining one side of Parade Loop are former Fort Walla Walla officers' residences. Some of the white clapboard houses built for officers' families were erected in 1858, making them the oldest homes in Walla Walla. The property is now part of the Wainwright Memorial VA Medical Center, and the former barracks have been repurposed for housing and offices. The entire military post with the original fort buildings is listed in the National Register of Historic Places. (Past image, Whitman College Archives.)

Running between Isaacs Avenue and University Street, Fulton Street is one of the shortest streets in Walla Walla. It is only one block long, with 14 homes. Most of the Fulton Street homes were built between 1905 and 1913 and were part of the Brookside Park Addition platted in 1905 by Lucie Fulton Isaacs, the widow of mill owner H.P. Isaacs. It is likely that Lucie named the street in honor of her pioneering Fulton family. (Past image, Whitman College Archives.)

The fire department is parading its teams and engines east on Alder Street in the 1908 image. The Denny and Drumheller Buildings still stand across from each other on Second Avenue, but the other structures on the south side of Alder Street are gone, including a house behind the trees that was the home of Walla Walla's most famous madame, Josephine Wolfe. Also razed was the fortress-like Betz Brewery on the southwest corner of Third Avenue. (Past image, Steve Wilen.)

Alder Street, Walla Walla, Wash.

This grand edifice, constructed in 1911 on the southwest corner of Main Street and Second Avenue, is the third Baker Boyer Bank building at this location. Long gone is the cabin of Hen Lee, Walla Walla's first Chinese resident, which was behind the first bank building on Alder Street in the 1860s. By the time of this past image, brick buildings had replaced the less substantial structures of Walla Walla's first Chinatown, which occupied Alder Street between First and Third Avenues. (Past image, Steve Wilen.)

9932. Baker-Boyer Bank Building, Walla Walla, Wash.

Whitman College,
Walla Walla, Washington

The past image from the turn of the 20th century shows Boyer Avenue, named for John Boyer of Baker Boyer Bank, which runs through the Whitman College campus. The building on the left is Memorial Hall. Seen in the distance is Billings Hall, which at the time was a dormitory and has now been replaced with a new structure. Due to more trees and fewer power poles, this stretch of Boyer Avenue is even more inviting today. (Past image, Steve Wilen.)

Projecting signs were popular on most main streets in the 1940s and 1950s, and Walla Walla was no exception. The Fuller Paints sign hung above the store on Main Street and First Avenue for over 25 years. During World War II, a temporary Victory Center stage was built next door to the paint store where visiting celebrities stood and urged crowds to buy war bonds. Today, a wine tasting room and framing studio occupy the Fuller space. (Past image, Fort Walla Walla Museum.)

On the northeast corner of Palouse and Birch Streets lived a prominent physician, Dr. Bingham, who established one of Walla Walla's first hospitals and was the author of papers on a variety of medical subjects. The horse and buggy in the past image would likely have been tied up using one of the metal rings embedded in the curb, a few of which still exist on Palouse Street today. (Past image, Steve Wilen.)

The group in the past image is assembled on Alder Street near Second Avenue and faces west. Walla Walla has several native tribes—Walla Walla, Cayuse, Umatilla, and Nez Perce—in the vicinity. It was not unusual for them to participate in pageants and events such as this Fourth of July parade in the early 1900s. Also seen in the photograph is the Dime Theater, which showed silent films. (Past image, Whitman College Archives.)

Die Brucke (German for "The Bridge") was so named because it was built next to the crossing for Mill Creek. No building stood on this spot until 1903 because the creek frequently overflowed its banks. Now diverted below the street, the creek runs under the building. From its beginning the building housed a bookstore; the popular Book Nook operated there for years. Today, an independent bookstore has its home at Die Brucke. (Past image, Fort Walla Walla Museum.)

PALOUSE STREET, A WALLA WALLA RESIDENCE STREET.

To see some of the most historic homes in Walla Walla, one should start at the intersection of Birch and Palouse Streets and walk south. The residences in this street scene were built on the west side of Palouse Street between 1907 and 1910 and were part of a development called the Roberts Addition. The homes were built on lots carved from vast tracts of fruit trees planted by A.B. Roberts in the 1860s. (Past image, Steve Wilen.)

During World War II, Walla Walla had a 2,164-acre Army air base where pilots were trained on B-17 and B-24 bombers. In the past photograph, townspeople watching a military parade are standing near the intersection of First Avenue and Main Street. The former Beehive Department Store on the corner is now a coffee shop. The four neighboring buildings have facades added in the 1960s and 1970s. (Past image, Fort Walla Walla Museum.)

The past photograph shows a brick building erected in 1889 on the southeast corner of Main Street and Fourth Avenue. Although it was built as a bank, the basement contained the considerable inventory of liquor dealer E. Le Boucher. Crescent Drugs occupied the building from 1920 to 1975, where Christopher Eubanks, a well-known pharmacist, offered his unique skin preparation known as Marvello. Today, it is the only building on the block from that era still standing. (Past image, Fort Walla Walla Museum.)

CHAPTER

5

HOMES

This grand house was home to two very prominent citizens. Dr. Nelson Gales Blalock was a physician who served two terms as mayor and was the founder of Blalock Orchards. John Dooley, known as "King Cattle," later bought the home for his bride, Frankie. The house stood on Second Avenue where the Marcus Whitman Hotel is now. (Whitman College Archives.)

William and Isabella Kirkman built their Victorian Italianate home in 1881 with F.P. Allen as their architect. William was a prosperous rancher who also had a meat market on Main Street. With the help of her Chinese domestic, Ah Sing, Isabella raised four children here. The home remained in the Kirkman family until 1923 when Isabella donated it to Whitman College, which used it briefly as a men's dormitory. Today, it is Kirkman House Museum. (Past image, Whitman College Archives.)

Dr. Suttner built this Neoclassical home in 1908 on the northwest corner of Palouse and Birch Streets. It was designed with a side entrance for Dr. Suttner's patients. Farmer William Struthers and his wife, Lucy, bought the mansion in 1905 and lived here until the 1930s. A boardinghouse for a while and then a mental health center, it is now beautifully restored and houses a law firm. (Past image, Whitman College Archives.)

In 1910, Alexander McDonald hired architect Charles Lambert to build this home with its distinctive swooping gables on Palouse Street. McDonald soon sold the house to Brewster and Caroline Ferrel, a farming family who arrived by mule team in 1864 and homesteaded on Russell Creek. A residence this large rarely remains a single-family home. As early as 1952, the Brewster Ferrel home was divided into apartments, which is still the case today. (Past image, Fort Walla Walla Museum.)

MODERN HOMES OF WALLA WALLA
Residence of Alexander McDonald, 336 Palouse St.   C. B. Lambert, builder.

Dr. James Cropp, who built this home on Rose Street in 1899, was a local physician who established Walla Walla Hospital. Built of Tenino stone, the mansion has an octagonal tower and a wraparound porch. Dr. Cropp married Ida Hungate, and with her and then with his second wife, Gertrude, lived here until 1923. Daughter Hattie made the mansion her home with her husband, postmaster George Day, until 1936. (Past image, Whitman College Archives.)

When he first came to Walla Walla in the 1860s, Maximillian Baumeister operated the Oriental Hairdressing and Shaving Saloon on Main Street. By 1896, Baumeister had amassed the fortune that allowed him to build this stately home, which he called Waldheim, with his wife, Alvina. Max died in 1909, and in 1914, Alvina decided to remodel, which is why Waldheim has no tower in the present photograph. Alvina lived here until her death in 1937. Waldheim is on the corner of Stone and Edwards Streets. (Past image, Julia and Roger Russell.)

RESIDENCE OF COL. F. J. PARKER.

Built in the 1880s, this Victorian Italianate home on Catherine Street was occupied by Col. Frank Parker and his family. Colonel Parker, editor of the local newspaper, the *Walla Walla Statesman,* probably paid to have this engraving of his home featured on an 1889 advertising map. By 1906, the house was home to a variety of boarders, including a clerk, a salesman, and a bartender, but since the 1920s, it has been a single-family home. (Past image, Whitman College Archives.)

Robert and Ferdinanda Horn built this Queen Anne–style house on South Third Avenue around 1900 and lived there for more than 20 years with their daughter Kittie. Ferdinanda was very active socially and held parties and women's auxiliary meetings at her home, at which she served "dainty" refreshments. Originally a watchmaker at Z.K. Straight Jewelers, Robert opened his own jewelry store in 1905. (Past image, Fort Walla Walla Museum.)

Louis Anderson, classics professor at Whitman College, married one of the wealthiest women in Walla Walla, Mabel Baker, and with her built this Classic Revival house on Boyer Avenue in 1903. Mabel died in 1915, and Louis's second wife, Florence, lived here until her death in 1968. The Andersons' Chinese servant Jim was not only an excellent cook but also landscaped the grounds of this home, which is now the faculty center for Whitman College. (Past image, Whitman College Archives.)

Phillip Ritz was renowned for his orchards and innovative horticulture and made a fortune in the nursery business. However, he died before his widow, Catherine, built this magnificent Queen Anne home in 1895. Standing in the midst of orchards, the house was named Ever Green Glen by Catherine. After Phillip's death, his nephew William married Hattie, the Ritzes' daughter. The couple and Catherine all lived in the mansion and carried on Phillip's business. (Past image, Whitman College Archives.)

HOMES

Stephen Penrose was the first Whitman College president to live in this 1921 home on Boyer Avenue, which was financed by alumni fundraising. He and his wife, May, raised six children here with the help of Hoy, their Chinese servant. May Penrose was very active in community causes and founded the local Young Women's Christian Association. Converted to college administrative offices in 1995, the building is called Penrose House in honor of its first residents. (Past image, Whitman College Archives.)

President's House Whitman College

In 1916, O.D. Keen, a local contractor, built this Neoclassical home for Ben and Bessie Grote. It stands on Birch Street at the north end of Catherine Street. Ben Grote, also known as "The Wheat King," was one of the first local farmers to utilize silos for grain storage and built two of the county's largest fireproof elevators. Ben died in 1946, but Bessie lived here as a widow until 1976. (Past image, Fort Walla Walla Museum.)

Sadie and R.B. Caswell built this Craftsman bungalow on Boyer Avenue in 1904. R.B. Caswell, a cigar store owner, is shown in the past photograph with his daughters Nadine (left) and Susanne. Dr. Elmer Hill and his wife, Bertha, moved into the home in the 1920s and lived there for nearly 30 years. After Elmer's death, it was an apartment house through the mid-1960s. Today, it is a bed and breakfast. (Past image, Penny Maxwell Bingham.)

Residence in Walla Walla, Wash.

This imposing bungalow on Newell Street was built in 1904 by George Ludwig, one of Walla Walla's first jewelry store owners. River rock from Mill Creek—80 wagonloads—were used to face the distinctive fence and house foundation. The home stands on a large lot, and Ludwig was famous for the huge apricots, as big as peaches, he grew in his backyard. The secret of his success, he said, was thinning every year. (Past image, Steve Wilen.)

Built in 1884 by Washington territorial governor Miles C. Moore and his wife, Molly, this home sits on four densely planted acres on Bryant Avenue. A creek runs through the property. The Queen Anne–style house was originally painted a subdued white and remained that way for decades until its purchase in the early 2000s, when it was transformed into a painted lady with eye-catching lively colors. (Past image, Whitman College Archives.)

Built in 1923, the Georgian-style Lyman House is the oldest residence hall on the Whitman College campus. It was named in honor of history professor and author William Denison Lyman, who taught at Whitman from 1889 until his death in 1920. Originally a men's residence, during World War II it housed V-12 trainees, who nicknamed it the "U.S.S. Lyman." It is now a coed, mixed-class hall housing 89 students. (Past image, Whitman College Archives.)

Lyman House Whitman College

C.B. Upton built this home in 1893, and he and his wife, Addie, began their marriage here. C.B. died in 1904, and his widow sold the home. By 1926, the new owner rented rooms, and a side wing of units was added in 1938. The apartment house had many names over the years, and in 1984, the building became Sharpstein Manor, named after Annabel Sharpstein, who owned the home in the 1930s and 1940s. (Past image, Whitman College Archives.)

Built in the early 1930s, the Washington Apartments were designed in the Art Deco style by local architect Victor Siebert. An ornamented round arch frames the entrance, which is set on the southeast corner of Birch Street and Second Avenue. Some of the 66 units retain a phone niche, and in some kitchens, there is original subway tile. The L-shaped building has five floors, and the original Otis elevator is still used. (Past image, Whitman College Archives.)

"Willie" Baker was active in the planning of this 1900 Colonial Revival–style house that he and his wife, Mary Esther, built on the corner of Craig and Park Streets. A son of banker Dorsey Baker, Willie was a successful entrepreneur himself; he established the Baker Loan and Investment Company. Mary Esther died in 1903, and Willie married her sister Emma, an avid gardener. Emma is probably the woman pictured in the past photograph. (Past image, Doug Saturno.)

This charming bungalow was built on Marcus Street in 1911 by Charles McEvoy and his wife, Pink. By 1920, Lincoln and Henrietta Baker Kennedy lived there. Henrietta was the granddaughter of Dorsey Baker, the entrepreneur responsible for the first railroad line that joined Walla Walla with the Columbia River. In 1965, the home was purchased by the fraternity Delta Tau Delta and was remodeled to accommodate 40 students. Today, it is student housing for Whitman College. (Past image, Steve Wilen.)

RESIDENCE, WALLA WALLA, WASH.

J.A. McLean was listed as a farmer in the 1904 directory, but by 1910, he had become a contractor and was responsible for building several attractive homes around town, including this Foursquare. Built in 1909 for himself and his wife, Mamie, it was one of the earliest to be erected on Alvarado Terrace and cost $4,000. After J.A. died in 1921, Mamie sold the house and moved into one nearby. (Past image, Fort Walla Walla Museum.)

The Seil family was known in Walla Walla as owners of a shoe store housed in a downtown building that still bears their name. A passerby of daughter Emma Seil's 1929 brick home on Palouse Street would not be surprised to hear that she was an admirer of Monticello. Portraits of US presidents lined the walls of the reception hall. Emma Seil died in 1969 after living in the home for 70 years. (Past image, Whitman College Library.)

Dewey and Bertha Drumheller's Colonial Revival home on First Avenue was built in 1918. Both Dewey and Bertha came from pioneering families, and Dewey was still roping cattle in his 50s, while Bertha's interests were gardening and serving as a hostess. The house was designed and built by Lambert and Bailey, a versatile architect and contractor team who were also responsible for the First Presbyterian Church to the north on the same block and a Craftsman bungalow to the south on Thorne Street. (Past image, Fort Walla Walla Museum.)

DISCOVER THOUSANDS OF LOCAL HISTORY BOOKS
FEATURING MILLIONS OF VINTAGE IMAGES

Arcadia Publishing, the leading local history publisher in the United States, is committed to making history accessible and meaningful through publishing books that celebrate and preserve the heritage of America's people and places.

Find more books like this at
www.arcadiapublishing.com

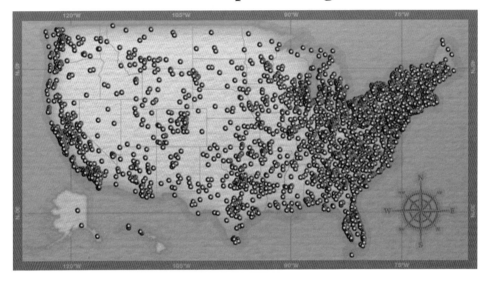

Search for your hometown history, your old stomping grounds, and even your favorite sports team.